THE CANARY
THAT
BARKED

Keith T. Weber

NOTE TO READERS
This publication contains the ideas and opinions of its author and is intended to provide information to the reader on the subjects dealt with in this book. It is provided with the understanding that the author and the publisher are not offering services of any kind in this book or associated website(s). The reader should carefully consult with his or her medical doctor before applying or adopting any suggestions in this book or drawing inferences based suggestions found in this book.

LIMIT OF LIABILITY/DISCLAIMER OF WARRANTY
While the publisher and author have used their best efforts in preparing this book, they make no representations or warranties with respect to the accuracy or completeness of the contents of the book and specifically disclaim any implied warranties of merchantability or fitness for a particular purpose. Neither the publisher nor author shall be liable for any loss or damages, incurred as a direct or indirect consequence of the use/application of any content, including but not limited to special, incidental, consequential, or other damages.

Copyright © 2014

Weber, Keith T., 1966-
    The Canary that Barked/by Keith T. Weber
    1.   Environment.   2. Health.

ISBN-13: 978-1499306057
ISBN-10: 1499306059

"The wise man understands that he is never done learning, always bettering himself. The fool believes he knows everything already."

-Thomas Jefferson

To all the wonderful dogs who have shared their lives with man across the centuries and especially those who have given their lives that we might live even one more day.

Contents

List of Illustrations

THE CANARY
THAT
BARKED

Chapter 1
-Romy-

Romy passed away on November 26th, 2005 at the tender age of four. I recall it every Thanksgiving because it was so near that Holiday. I guess one could say we anticipated his death as he was diagnosed with bone cancer a few months earlier. Saying we were ready for his death is altogether different and would be far from the truth as it felt like we had just lost a young child. The fact is we still miss him today.

Romy was a Great Pyrenees who was absolutely gentle and kind-hearted. If Romy had been a person I am certain he would have been the most humble and thoughtful person I ever met. I say that because it seemed like he put himself last in our family and not because he was timid but instead because he was brave and confident. The only way to truly understand this would have been for you to have met Romy, but since that is not possible, let me relate a story that in many ways captures the essence of who Romy was.

The American Temperament Testing Society (ATTS) has developed a series of evaluations to determine a dog's temperament relative to its breed standard. Using this approach, the ATTS tester does not expect a Shih Tzu to behave like a Rottweiler and vice versa. Intrigued by ATTS' method, we entered Romy in a test and because Great Pyrenees are a guardian breed, we were curious how he would respond to the final test, the "aggressive stranger".

If you know Great Pyrenees then you know these dogs have been bred for centuries to protect sheep from predators with their first line of defense being barking. Usually that is all it takes as the predator figures out he has been detected and the entire pasture is now on high-alert. If barking does not work, a good guardian will escalate the threat to include more aggressive barking (increased volume with decreased wavelength of barks (i.e., lower and louder barking)) and physical posturing. Ultimately, and only if necessary, will the guardian resort to a physical attack.

When it came our turn for the test, Romy and I marched out and started making our rounds. The stations flew by and everything was going very well; the neutral stranger, the friendly stranger, the odd sounds, the unusual footing and so on. Romy was so calm it seemed like the tests had no effect on him, I guess he thought we were just out for a walk in the park. The aggressive stranger was next as we arrived at our designated stopping point. There came a loud and nasty sounding voice --close, about 50 feet away. Romy paid close attention, his eyes fixed in that direction. Then a stranger appeared from behind some bushes. He didn't look at all friendly and kept hollering, moving closer toward us and waving a club. Romy put himself between me and the stranger and stood his ground, so big, brave and proud! When the threat continued and the stranger came too close, Romy moved forward again, as far as the lead would allow, and let out a series of deep, powerful barks.

The stranger left and Romy kept his eyes on him all the while. There was not a better response to be had from a guardian dog and it was clear Romy was ready to lay down his own life so that mine could be spared. Needless to say, Romy passed the test.

--

Dogs are a special part of the lives of many Americans and sad stories, just like Romy's battle with cancer, are all too familiar. As a scientist I have been trained to be skeptical of lay person observations and to forever question assumed truths. It is that background that set me on a path to better understand cancer in dogs and ultimately the role the environment plays in our own health. The result, nearly a decade later is this book.

This book is not so much about dogs as it is about the environment we share with our dogs. It's about human health, food security, consumer buying power, and our future. The first three chapters share some stories with you as we prepare a case to scrutinize and review the evidence that something may be going awry with our environment. It's not an easy case, as you will see, and in the end you may not know much more than you do right now. It is my hope however, to connect a lot of seemingly disparate threads into a cohesive case that indicts not big business or corporate America, nor the government, but us, all of us.

--

I was at a science conference some years ago when a colleague whom I had not seen in quite some time approached me and asked "whaddya know Keith?" My answer of "less and less each day" took him by surprise. You see, I was not joking about getting old and becoming forgetful (though that may be true too) but rather I was condensing recent reflections into a single thought.

That is, the number of things that I *unquestionably know* to be true is fewer and fewer each day.

Think about it. How often have you heard or read some bold statement about A causes B only to find out later the statement should have been A *may* cause B, if conditions C, D and E are also true. Cancer causing foods and beverages are great examples. In the 1970's saccharin made the headlines when scientists were quoted to say "saccharin causes cancer"[1]. If you remember this then you might also remember some of the details that came out later; the fact this claim was based on experiments with laboratory rats (and not human cancer cases) which were fed enormous quantities of refined saccharin, resulting in many of these rats (but not all) developing cancer. The take home message is that saccharin use may lead to cancer but it is not true to say it *will* cause cancer.

The broader lesson here is that as readers, consumers, and parents we need to be far more critical of the truisms so readily broadcast today. We need to seek credible references and based on that information decide, as Robert Ripley would say, to believe it or not.

--

Cancer is a strange disease in that it cannot be transmitted from one person to another. Indeed there really is no transmission of cancer; no insects, fleas, bacteria, or viruses. Instead cancer is almost like a self-destruct disorder within the body. There is clearly a genetic pre-condition to cancer as the make-up of a given individual may contain cancer suppressor genes or it may not. Hence those individuals with one genetic makeup may not contract cancer, while another will, even when both live in the same environment.

[1] See http://en.wikipedia.org/wiki/Saccharin

In dogs, cancer has become a leading cause of death for nearly all breeds. The American Veterinary Medical Association (AVMA) reports cancer kills nearly 50% of dogs over the age of 10. In 2007 the Morris Animal Foundation cited 25% of all dog deaths are due to cancer. This is likely as precise as canine cancer statistics get since it is so difficult to assemble more meaningful data. Certainly not all dogs that die of cancer are diagnosed and as a result those deaths are not included in any direct count. This does not suggest the AVMA and Morris Foundation reports underestimate canine cancer though, as these organizations have likely made efforts to account for these uncertainties in their calculations and reports.

Luckily, there is much better data describing cancer in humans and these data can be pretty sobering. Imagine if you will that we are transported back to 2005, the same year Romy passed away. Further imagine that you and 215 other people are comfortably seated in a stadium. An announcer's voice calls out the name of just one of these 216 people. Next, fast-forward to the end of 2012 and once again you find yourself in the same stadium along with just 190 other people. The announcer again selects one from the crowd. Those people who were selected and made the final cut were not the lucky ones; instead they represent new cancer cases for that year. Which scenario do you prefer, the one from 2005 or the one from 2012? In other words, do you prefer a 1 in 216 chance of getting cancer or a 1 in 191 chance (Figure 1-1)?

What is particularly interesting about these statistics is the increased likelihood that you (or I) will get cancer compared to what it was less than a decade ago[2]. Indeed, while America's population grew approximately 6% between 2005 and 2012, new

---

[2] Bear in mind, these statistics are not cancer deaths, but rather the number of new cancer cases reported each year.

cancer cases rose 19% over that same time period. Proportionally, new cancer cases are outpacing population growth at a rate of 3:1.

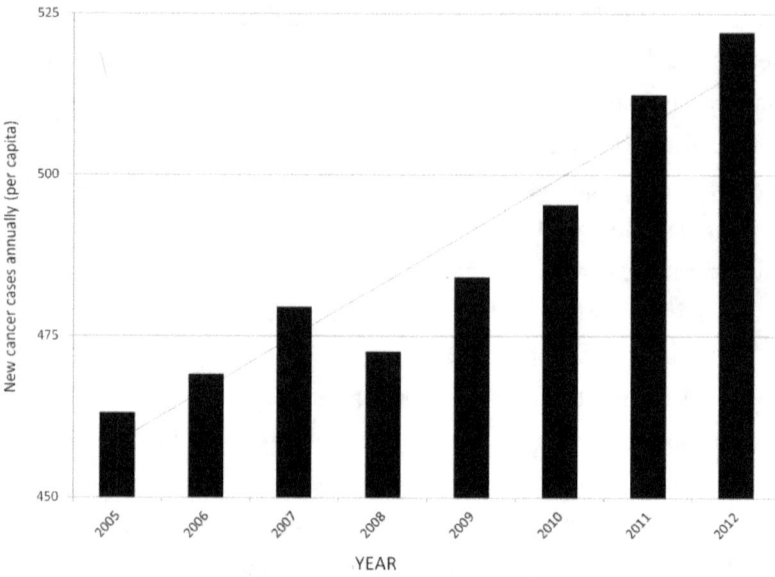

Figure 1- 1 The increasing rate of new cancer cases in America between 2005 and 2012. These data have been adjusted for America's growing population by dividing the number of new cancer cases by the nation's population for that year, and then displaying the results in a familiar per capita fashion (x 100,000). The long-term trend is shown by the dotted line.

Data source: American Cancer Society

Even more important than these statistics is a question about our future. But before offering a forecast, let's first consider the applicability of these historical data for future prediction. To do this we will use a calculation that is commonly used to describe the reliability of a trend line. This value is called R^2 (read R-squared) and a perfect R^2 has a value of 1.00. The R^2 for *our* data is 0.92, or 92% certain that our trend line fits the actual historic data. With such a high R^2 value, we can feel confident that extrapolating (or extending) the trend into the future will yield equally reliable answers. The result of this gloomy forecast suggests that one in every 160 Americans will be diagnosed with cancer by the year 2020.

Why is this happening? It is without question that our knowledge about cancer has grown (and continues to grow). It is also clear that our knowledge of preventive medicine and healthy lifestyles has similarly improved. The Mayo clinic and US Centers for Disease Control and Prevention (CDC) both report that dietary supplement use, especially multivitamins, has increased, and today more than half of Americans are taking some form of vitamin or mineral supplement (see chapter six for a more detailed look at dietary supplements). Overall, many American's are *trying* to live healthier lifestyles as the number of adults who smoke continues to decline (from 21% in 2005 to 19% in 2010) and nutritional awareness is improving. So what is going on? What is happening here in America --and very likely across the globe-- that is at the core of this very real health problem?

Chapter 2
-Julie-

Julie is a dog. She is another of our Great Pyrenees and like so many other dogs; she has her own special "personality" (or dog-ality perhaps). If Julie were a person, she would be a Diva. Rightly so, perhaps, as her accolades include not only earning a Champion title from the American Kennel Club (AKC) but also a Versatility Ambassador (VA) title and, like Romy, a Temperament Test (TT) title as well. Add to all this, the fact Julie starred in a Eukanuba commercial and one could argue she is well within her rights to be a Diva. But, for the great majority of her life outside the limelight, Julie has been a wonderful pet and member of our family.

They say Great Pyrenees (Pyrs for those in the know) are like potato chips, you can't stop with just one, and so a few years ago we got the bright idea we should breed Julie. We selected a wonderful mate for her; one that we hoped would help create another generation of fantastic dogs that, like Julie and Romy, would make wonderful pets and family members.

Pardon the pun, but we had a dog of a time producing a litter of puppies. Through this experience we discovered Julie had "messed up" heat cycles and learned more about mammalian reproduction than we ever dreamed. You see, ovulation in dogs occurs when estrogen levels achieve a specific threshold. Typical outwardly apparent "heat cycle" behavior on the other hand begins at much lower estrogen levels. For most bitches (a female canine) estrogen levels increase steadily along a well understood path and ovulation can be expected approximately 10 days after "spotting" is noted. Julie's estrogen levels however followed a more undulating or wavy path and did not result in ovulation until nearly 30 days after spotting was first noticed. Only by working closely with a respected canine reproductive specialist were we able to learn all this and eventually manage to produce a litter of precious little Pyr puppies.

While Julie was a great mom to those puppies, there comes a time in a bitch's life when it's best to spay her and thereby reduce the likelihood of certain types of cancer. So a few years after she had her litter, Julie was spayed. When we returned to the vet's office to pick her up that day, we were informed that while the procedure went well, they found her uterus was filled with fibroid cysts. Almost instantly then, the difficulties we had with her "messed-up" heat cycles began to make sense.

--

Uterine fibroid cysts are non-cancerous tumors that grow within the walls of the uterus. It is likely the condition can exist in any mammals and certainly does occur in both dogs and humans. Some women afflicted with uterine fibroids exhibit no outward indications while others experience tremendous pain and discomfort. Studies suggest a genetic linkage and perhaps even a racial predisposition for the disorder. More recent studies have demonstrated the role reproductive hormones have on the growth of uterine fibroids with estrogen itself acting as a growth stimulant.

Uterine fibroids have also been linked to various fertility problems and for some women, it has become necessary to first remove then uterine fibroids to subsequently allow them to conceive and have children.

Knowing this, it was easier to understand why Julie had problems conceiving her litter of puppies. Outside of her heat cycle Julie surely still had fibroids, but since there was effectively no estrogen to stimulate their growth, no problems were encountered. Once her estrogen levels began to rise however, growth of the uterine fibroids was consequently accelerated, thereby complicating and potentially prohibiting implantation of a fertilized egg onto the wall of the uterus. "Bingo", I thought to myself, "I am beginning to understand".

Just understanding is not enough however as this problem is far broader in its scope. Fibroids are the cause of approximately 50% of the half-million hysterectomies performed on American women each year. The prevalence of fibroids does not have a well-documented history and since the 1990's, the same statistic has been repeatedly cited (e.g., 600,000 hysterectomies are performed each year with approximately half of these due to complications caused by uterine fibroids). If this were accurate, then the problem is declining since the US population has increased substantially over that same time period (248 million in 1990 to over 314 million in 2012). However, a study published in 2012 paints a different picture, revealing that nearly 7% of American women have uterine fibroids[3].

Let's extrapolate this information to the broader US population to better understand the magnitude of the problem. As

[3] http://www.ncbi.nlm.nih.gov/pmc/articles/PMC3342149/

noted above, there was an estimated 314 million people in America in 2012. Slightly over half of these (51%) are women, with approximately 65 million of reproductive age (15-44). This is the demographic of concern for uterine fibroids. If we assume 7% of these women have this condition that equals 4.6 million women. If we further extrapolate this and recognize that currently the only "cure" for uterine fibroids is hysterectomy, then we begin to approach a true appreciation of the problem.

--

Regardless of the specifics of any problem, all problems are dealt with following one of two basic solution pathways 1) reactive or 2) proactive. Hysterectomy is a reactive solution to a problematic uterine fibroid condition. An arguably better solution would follow a proactive pathway where prevention is fundamental. However, to *prevent* something we first need to know its *cause*.

This opens an entirely new discourse as the cause for widespread uterine fibroid disorders is not clear. Currently a genetic predisposition is suspect with disproportionately higher number of cases seen in African American women in some age classes. In addition, diet seems to play a role as studies reported by the National Institutes of Health (NIH) suggest consumption of dairy products and green tea may help reduce uterine fibroid problems.

In contrast, other foods act to increase estrogen levels or even mimic estrogen in the body. Soy products are a good example as soybeans contain relatively high levels of phytoestrogens (plant-based estrogen-like compounds). In addition, various vegetables like black-eyed peas contain high levels of estrogen promoting substances as do flax seeds, sunflower seeds, and citrus fruits. Herbal supplements like Dong quai and black cohosh are taken by many women specifically to stimulate estrogen production, though their efficacy has not been proven. This is not to suggest women should avoid all these nutritious foods but rather, I believe this list and brief discussion serves to illustrate that diet is likely not the primary cause of the problem and indeed the role diet plays is likely minimal.

Instead we need to look at xenoestrogens. Similar to the phytoestrogens described earlier, xenoestrogens are artificial, chemical compounds that imitate estrogen in the body. While not developed or produced by design, xenoestrogens are widespread and can be found in items we use or consume every day, such as food additives (preservatives such are Propyl gallate and 4-hexylresorcinol) and industrial products like Bisphenol A (BPA). BPA can be found not only in plastic[4] water bottles but in the thermal paper used to print nearly all cash register receipts used in America today.

Table 2- 1 A partial list of common xenoestrogens

Atrazine (herbicide)
BPA (plastics)
Dioxin (paper production)
Endosulfan (insecticide)
4-Methylbenzylidene camphor (sunscreen lotion)
4-hexylresorcinol (food preservative)
Parabens (cosmetic lotions)
Propyl gallate (food preservative)

While it would seem that BPA is harmlessly bound up inside plastic, a 2007 study demonstrated that BPA is released by detergents, acid, and heat. In other words, the high-acid sodas and fruit juices we drink from plastic bottles and the foods we heat in

---

[4] Plastics marked as type 03 and 07 may contain BPA.

some microwave-safe plastic containers may contain a dose of BPA that will be ingested into our bodies just as readily as the left-overs and soda used to wash it all down. Furthermore, a 2006 expert panel concluded that BPA levels in humans were above those known to cause problems in laboratory animals (to keep this all in proper perspective though, please recall the saccharin scare described in chapter one).

BPA, along with a host of other xenoestrogens (Table 2-1), have been connected to early on-set of puberty as well as other reproductive disorders in both women and men. This then brings us full-circle, as early on-set of puberty (precocious puberty) is well correlated with uterine fibroids and while perhaps not the proverbial smoking gun, it is certainly something worthy of our attention as we continue connecting threads the better understand the environment we have created for ourselves.

Chapter 3
-The Oldest Puppy Ever-

Simon was a 130 pound furry bundle of happiness with a joy-filled spirit that was contagious. If you ever felt down all you had to do was visit Simon and you could not help but feel happy. To me he was the "oldest puppy ever"... even when he was over four years old. He played with his toys, and left them strewn about the yard, he played with us, and he played with Julie, his Mom.

Simon was one of those dogs that loved everyone and tried to make friends with anyone he met, including the neighbor's cattle and horses. His charm was apparently irresistible and many of his friends also fell in love with him and found themselves *Simon-ized* as we called it.

When Simon was three, he began having occasional seizures and when they became more severe, he was put on medication to control them. The medication made no difference in his character; he was still the same happy, loving puppy.

On a sunny Father's day afternoon I went out on the patio to spend some time with both Simon and Julie. I sat and rubbed them both and since it was quite hot, Simon decided it was time for a nap. He laid down at my feet and fell asleep. I remember thinking "this is a very nice Father's day", the weather was nice, all my chores were done, and now I am simply relaxing. And with my dogs resting at my feet, it really was a great day.

A few minutes later, I placed Simon's favorite ducky pillow beneath his head and went back inside to refill my glass of water. When I returned I saw Simon was having a seizure. It was a small one. But then another came and another. We took Simon to the vet and it seemed the seizures would not stop. The vet tried everything she could, including massive doses of anti-seizure medicine. Nothing worked.

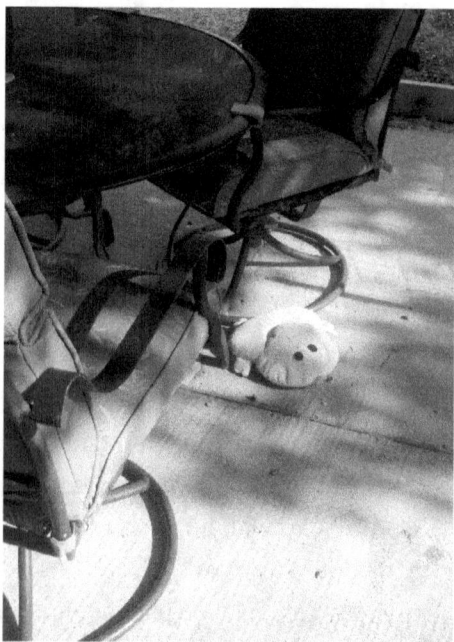

Figure 3- 1 It is likely that Simon's last lucid memories happened right here while we enjoyed a nice summer afternoon together

We were with Simon when he passed away at about 4pm, Monday June 17th, 2013, crying and saying goodbye. If you are not a "dog-person" you may have trouble understanding the emotional bond that is formed between a dog and "dog-person". I cannot even attempt to describe it short of saying dog become part of our family. Losing a dog, like any other family member, is terribly difficult.

--

Let's rewind this story now and focus on seizures as a health condition. First, it is important to understand that seizure disorder (or epilepsy) is not a disease, but rather the expression of an underlying problem. In both humans and dogs, the problem is often related to neurological diseases, brain injuries, or brain tumors. Like many other health conditions, seizure disorders appear to have strong genetic linkages as well.

Knowing this, we were well prepared, albeit apprehensive, for our first visit to the vet after Simon first starting having seizures. Unfortunately, the litany of tests and blood chemistry showed no indications of neurological diseases, brain injuries, or tumors. What's more, we were told our experience was not out of the ordinary as identifying the "underlying problem" is not always simple. Since a definitive somatic basis for Simon's seizures could not be isolated, we began focusing on preventing addition seizures. At the doctor's urging we began taking careful notes about conditions during and immediately preceding a seizure event that might help isolate the trigger in Simon's environment. Unfortunately, no clear trends emerged and to us, it seemed like something was building up in his system and "erupting" every 40 days or so. When his seizures became more prevalent (more than once per month) he was placed on anti-seizure medication (phenobarbital) to help control this disorder.

We never did learn what caused Simon's seizures other than being told it was most likely something in his environment that his body was sensitized or hyper-sensitized to. And that is why

Simon's story is part of this book. His health condition was not caused by a tumor or a genetic defect, but for all the medical science in the world, the best we can say is his seizures --and ultimately his death-- was caused by the environment.

We hear this far too often today as nearly every poorly understood disease or disorder is attributed to genetics and the environment. I am not arguing this is wrong but rather, agreeing and suggesting the environment in which we live has profound effects on our health. If you really consider this it becomes almost silly to think otherwise. That little sphere of air that surrounds our bodies every moment of our lives since birth is constantly bathing our skin with the same atmosphere we breathe. While the atmosphere is principally composed of nitrogen (approximately 78%) and oxygen (approximately 21%) it can also contain water vapor and pollutants. The skin we once considered an impenetrable barrier to all things smaller than a hornet's stinger is now understood to be a semi-permeable tissue that can absorb a host of nasty chemicals. In fact, recent research is beginning to suggest that chemicals absorbed through the skin are more of a health concern than ever thought before. The reasoning is this; harmful substances that enter the body through our food and drink are often filtered out by the liver and kidneys. In contrast substances absorbed through the skin bypass the digestive system and enter the bloodstream intact. Just one class of substances of increasing concern is the xenoestrogens common in sunscreens and skin lotions (see chapter two). Looking beyond the lotions that we intentionally slather on our skin is also important, and prompts the question of what other airborne substances are our bodies exposed to?

The US Environmental Protection Agency (EPA) warns us about six common air pollutants that primarily enter our bodies through respiration and include ground-level ozone, particulate matter, and nitrogen dioxide. Being at the top of the EPA's list, ground-level ozone[5] is formed through a chemical reaction between two airborne pollutants, Nitrogen dioxide and various volatile organic compounds (VOC) commonly found in the emissions of some industrial plants as well as from internal combustion engines. This reaction is catalyzed through heat making ground-level ozone more problematic during hot summer weather. Once formed, this pollutant irritates the entire respiratory system and can actually cause permanent lung damage.

Ultraviolet radiation is emitted from the sun and passes through our atmosphere and ultimately, onto us. According to WebMD, UV (in any form, including tanning salons) is the single most important cause of skin cancer. The US Centers for Disease Control (CDC) goes on to warn us that UV rays (principally UVA rays) can penetrate into the skin and change skin cells.

No one wants to live their life wearing a full-body biochemical suit and indeed no one should even consider such unnecessary action. Indeed the World Health Organization (WHO) reminds us that exposure to the sun's rays (including small amounts of UV) is necessary for the body to produce vitamin D, which is critical to healthy bones and our overall health.

The point we need to recognize, or the thread we need to pick up, is that our entire environment may itself be the primary basis for some of the health problems we are seeing today. Our atmosphere and our environment may be hyper-sensitizing certain segments of our population to substances associated with commonly used goods and products like milk (according to the CDC, food allergies have increased 18% from 1997 to 2007) and peanut butter (peanut allergies have doubled between 1997 and

---

[5] For more information visit
http://www.epa.gov/airquality/ozonepollution/pdfs/ozonegb.pdf

2003). What's more, even 14% of dogs suffer from skin allergies. While I am not blaming any specific pollutant or contaminant, I am suggesting the need for additional research focused on environmental hyper-sensitization[6] which may ultimately help explain many allergies, severe reactions, and perhaps even the trigger for environmentally-linked seizure disorders.

---

[6] I am not suggesting or insinuating global warming is connected to the environmental issues described in this book. For a more in-depth discussion on the issues of climate and long-term climatic oscillations read Anatoly M. Khazanov's *Nomads and the Outside World* and *Climate Change Reconsidered* which is available from the Heartland Institute's website (http://heartland.org).

Progress...

Historians and Biblical scholars tell us the prophet Daniel lived to the age of 90 and Ramses the Great, lived to approximately 85 years of age[1].

How does that compare to our current life expectancy? Interestingly enough the CDC estimates the average life expectancy of Americans is 78.7 years. At face value, that's an entire decade less than Daniel who walked this earth around 600 BC. Certainly, one could argue the validity of these figures, but I will rely upon the better judgment of our historians to settle that argument.

One could also argue these are rare cases of longevity and would be better compared to current rare cases like Jeanne Louise Calment who lived 122 years. With no offense intended, Ms. Calment lived only 30 years longer than Daniel and during an age of science and technology, that is hardly remarkable progress.

Others might point out that due to their positions, both Daniel and Ramses would have had access to the best medical care available and are not representative of their cohort populations. But then again, the best medical care in 600 BC (Daniel) or 1200 BC (Ramses) would be laughable compared to today's standards and certainly cannot explain the observed lack of change in life expectancy.

Something happened between then and now. By Jesus' time, life expectancy had dropped to about 40 and by 1900 it was only 47 here in America. Since that time life expectancy has slowly climbed at a rate of 2% per year to reach the current value of 78.

Today, what we consider progress are those things that improve our gross national product, our military might, and our leisurely distractions. Perhaps our fragile bodies were not designed to live much beyond 80, or perhaps we have been following the wrong path of progress all along.

1- Budge, E. A. W. 1989. The Mummy; A History of the Extraordinary Practices of Ancient Egypt. Bell Publishing Co. New York 404pp.

Chapter 4
-The Canary That Barked-

Scottish physiologist John Haldane pioneered the use of animal sentinels to protect miners from carbon monoxide in the 1890's. His approach was simple enough; use an animal that is *more* susceptible to a given environmental condition than we are (e.g., poison gas build-up) and if the animal dies in that environment, we can assume that environment is unsafe for humans as well. His approach was so effective that it actually remained in use until the 1980's.

For a variety of reasons, the canary was often the animal sentinel of choice. Presumably this was because its near-constant singing and chirping did not require a miner to frequently check-up on the sentinel. If the bird stopped singing it was usually reason enough to prompt an immediate evacuation of the mine.

Even though use of Haldane's idea seems to have died out, it may not be obsolete yet. Surely, the astute reader knows where I am going with this as chapters one and two described parallels between canine diseases and human diseases. Similarly, chapter three explored the complexities of atmospheric contaminants, hyper-sensitization, and the myriad connections between our environment and our health. In essence, the analogies I have described thus far make our dogs our own animal sentinels.

This may indeed be the perfect experiment just waiting to be analyzed. Like the canary in the coal mine, dogs tend to be *more* susceptible to many environmental contaminants than adult humans simply because 1) dogs are usually smaller in size and 2) dogs age more rapidly. Let's discuss each of these further before moving on.

The fact that most adult dogs are smaller than most adult humans is pretty obvious. Even giant breeds like the Great Pyrenees only weigh 100-150 lbs. and because of this, the actual amount of a contaminant or poison required to kill a dog is typically less than in humans[7]. This is referred to as the lethal dose (LD) and is quantified by toxicologists as LD_{50}, the lethal dose required to kill 50% of a given population. For many pathogens, substances, contaminants, and poisons the LD_{50} required to kill a dog is simply lower than for humans.

The latter point regarding aging is also important but perhaps not as apparent. Indeed, the fact that dogs have shorter lifespans *could* suggest they will be less likely to contract a disease simply because they don't live long enough to be exposed to the disease. On the surface this sounds pretty logical and may be true in instances of epidemics and plagues (an individual dog is less likely to be alive during these rare and episodic events) and for seasonal illnesses like influenza (a dog will experience fewer seasonal waves). To better understand how the dog's inherently

---

[7] This is not always the case however as dogs are far more sensitive to sodium, antioxidants, and various other substances. These are exceptions to the rule.

shorter lifespan relates to diseases like cancer however, means we need to consider the metabolism.

Without delving into the physiological equations used to calculate and model metabolism, suffice it to say that life expectancy exhibits an inverse relationship with metabolism, or more correctly, basal metabolic rate (BMR). In short, with all other things being equal, big animal species tend to live longer[8].

To get a better handle on metabolism and make a meaningful comparison between dogs and people, let's estimate maintenance energy requirement (MER) in Calories. This number can be pretty well refined if we know something about an individual's lifestyle and activity levels. To put all this into perspective we will compare the MER for a 150 pound adult man to that of a 150 pound adult dog (Table 4-1).

Table 4- 1 Comparing Maintenance Energy Requirements (MER) of humans and dogs

MER (in Calories [Kcal])	
150 lbs. adult man	2200
150 lbs. adult dog	3100

As shown in Table 4-1, the MER for the dog is 40% more than for a similarly sized human. In other words, we can consider dogs to have a 40% faster metabolism. As a result, the dog's longevity is reduced because the higher metabolism accelerates the body's rate of deterioration over time. While a 40% faster metabolism only partially explains differences in life expectancy, it clearly demonstrates dogs' age more rapidly than people.

[8] This is not entirely correct. For a more detailed discussion see http://en.wikipedia.org/wiki/Basal_animal_metabolic_rate

Let's return then to our original treatise that dogs may be near-perfect animal sentinels; they are susceptible to many of the same contaminants as people and unlike the canary, dogs are mammals and biologically a whole lot more similar to people than are birds. Secondly, it is significant that dogs share their lives with nearly 50% of Americans[9]. This means dogs live in the same homes, play in the same back yards, visit the same parks, and ride in the same automobiles. It also means dogs share many of the same foods with us; from leftovers to junk food.

These similarities really are important because it means our dogs are exposed to basically the same environment as we are 365 days each year. The same cannot be said about cats however -- which share their homes with 37% of Americans—as cats are far more carnivorous and usually less than excited about a morning walk or accompanying you for a ride down to the pet store.

Furthermore, the sheer numbers of dogs sharing their lives with people should not be overlooked. In science sample size is important and always scrutinized. The reasoning is very well understood and documented within the field of statistics, which in essence says that one observation (a very small sample size) of a person dying immediately after eating their favorite candy bar is most likely a coincidence and not proof of any causal relationship. However, if millions of people (a large sample size) die immediately after eating that same type of candy bar, the likelihood of causality rises tremendously. It is for these reasons -- and the close kinship we have with dogs -- that I believe it is perfectly legitimate to ask: what is it that our dogs are trying to tell us about the environment?

---

[9] http://media.americanpetproducts.org/press.php?include=144262

Chapter 5
-The Impact Sphere-

The term *sphere of influence*, or SOI, describes the geospatial region over which a nation exerts control or dominance. For example, the US has an enormous SOI politically, militarily, and economically relative to Turkmenistan[10]. The same term has also been applied to the retail world where a shopping center may be said to have an SOI over a geographic area. Similarly, the term *regional influence* has been used to indicate effectively the same concept. One could argue an individual also has a SOI as a mom or dad exerts parental control over their children and a CEO exerts dominance over his or her employees.

While SOI is an interesting topic, spending too much time in this discussion will lead us astray from the focus of this chapter. Thus, our discussion of SOI has served its purpose by introducing

[10] Central Asia's nation of Turkmenistan is considered one of the least known countries in the world.

a concept and providing a very nice segue into a related, albeit nearly opposite (yet highly applicable) concept; the *personal impact sphere*.

While this term was coined specifically for this book, rest assured my choice of words was not taken lightly. Numerous hours were spent poring over dictionaries and thesauruses, along with discussions with colleagues in geography. For the purposes of this book, the term *personal impact sphere* is defined as the effect a geographic region has on a person.

A similar, although simpler concept is MyEnvironment; a website[11] created and maintained by the United States Environmental Protection Agency (EPA). MyEnvironment was designed to provide Americans with environmental information about the area in which they live. This useful website serves as a springboard to help us think about the impact the immediate environment has on our health and well-being. Its shortcoming however is its somewhat over-simplified approach and omission of personal choice. Let me explain with a scenario.

> Both John Smith and Mary Doe are residents of Belle Fourche, South Dakota (the geographic center of the US). If both visit MyEnvironment's website they will both receive identical reports for their environment: air, water, energy, health, land, and community. This is misleading however, because John is a gardener and avid supporter of the local farmer's market. He is also a health conscious consumer who spends more time reading nutrition labels than the he does the local newspaper. Mary on the other hand is a free-spirit; a happy-go-lucky gal, who rarely

---

[11] Visit this website at http://www.epa.gov/myenvironment/ and learn more about your environment.

cooks a meal at home and instead, likes to grab a bite to eat at the nearest drive through restaurant.

Hence, there is more to your *personal impact sphere* than just what is found at your ZIP code and while the differences in the choices made by John and Mary may seem trivial, time has proven that everyday lifestyle-type choices have substantial ramifications on one's health. I am not dismissing the affect local environmental factors have on our health but rather, striving to take a holistic approach to health by highlighting the impact of all our decisions. For example, consider the fact that people who read nutrition labels eat 5% less fat. Obviously, it's not "reading labels" that makes the difference but instead the type of person that finds value in nutrition labels. This same type of person is also more likely to exercise and seek healthy choices in many of their daily decisions.

Returning to our earlier scenario, if both John and Mary visited MyEnvironment and studied the MyMaps and MyHealth sections, they would see their 2005 estimated cancer hazard quotient was 17 cases per million (Figure 5-1). Putting this into perspective, Belle Fourche's 17 falls well below the national average of 30, suggesting this city offers a nice environment and may be a pretty healthy place to live.

Is there a difference between the foods we buy at the local mega-mart (Mary's choice) and those we pick from our backyard garden(John's choice)? I mean, apart from taste --which one may argue is a purely subjective value anyway-- is there really a difference? If the number of calories and the grams of each vitamin and mineral were the same, do you believe each is equally healthy for you? I believe the gut-felt reaction across the US is that home-grown foods are intrinsically healthier for you, and surely part of the reasoning behind this has to do with residue.

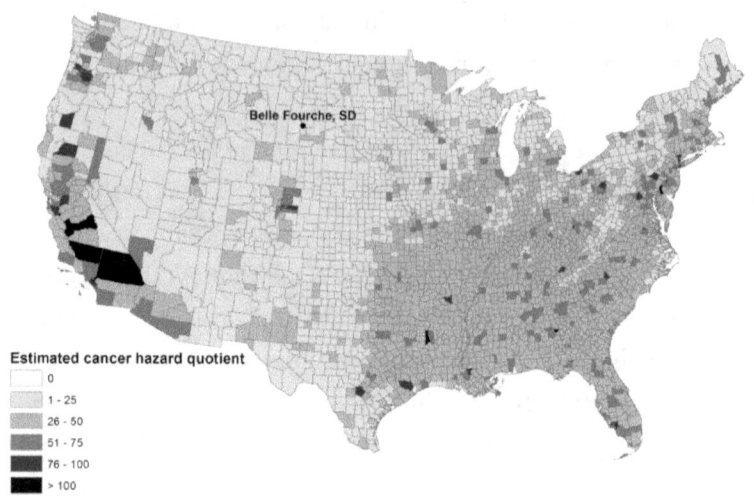

Figure 5- 1 EPA-estimated cancer hazard quotient for each US county. Belle Fourche should expect 17 cases per million which compares favorably against the national average of 30

Data source: National-Scale Air Toxics Assessment (NATA)

-Much Ado about Residue-

Pesticide residues have concerned many health-conscious consumers for decades and in response, the US Food and Drug Administration (FDA) began a pesticide monitoring program in 1987. This program samples and monitors pesticide residues in many of the food stuffs consumed across America, comparing measured pesticide residues against established safety standards[12]. The FDA's most recent Pesticide Monitoring Program report (2010) found only 2% of domestic foods and 5% of imported foods contained excessive levels of pesticide residues.

---

[12] Please note there is ongoing debate arguing the established safety standards allow excessive and unsafe levels of pesticide residues in our food supply.

Being a largely temperate climate, the US cannot grow all the fresh fruits and vegetables demanded by today's consumer throughout the year. For instance, to meet consumer demands for fresh mango in February, today's grocers need to import foods from other nations. To do so, fresh fruits like mango need to be picked well before they are ripe. The difficulty associated with such an early harvest is most fruits and vegetables simply will not ripen naturally when picked so early. To remedy this, ethylene gas is used to force-ripen the produce[13].

While there are no known health concerns associated with ethylene gas and force-ripened fruits and vegetables, the same is not true of the farming practices used in many of the foreign countries where our winter-time fresh fruits and vegetables originate. Indeed, 25% of all fresh and frozen produce sold in the US is imported. In fact, since 2005 the US has become a net importer of food following a long-term agricultural trade balance decline. While the US enjoyed a nearly $14 billion positive agricultural trade balance in 2001, within four years the scales tipped as the result of our nation's appetite for yearlong fresh produce and exotic foodstuffs. In raw tonnage however, the US is still a net exporter with nearly 170 million metric tons of food exported (2013) compared to only 55 million metric tons imported. What we are exporting are relatively inexpensive foods (e.g., grains) while we import expensive fruits, wines, and cheeses, hence the trade balance deficit.

One of our primary trade partners is Mexico and approximately 50% of imported produce originates just south of our border. While reliable statistics describing the type and amount of pesticides applied in foreign countries is difficult to determine,

---

[13] The use of ethylene gas to force-ripen produce has never been shown to pose any health risk to consumers.

some generalities may be applied to better understand what we are biting into.

1) Pesticides banned in the US may still be used in other countries. This includes DDT (which remains in use in both India and Brazil), 2,4,5-T (i.e., Agent Orange), and Parathion.

2) The rate of pesticide application is frequently much higher in countries like Mexico and China relative to the rate of pesticide application in the US. For example, an average of nearly two pounds of pesticide is applied per acre in the US, while Chinese farmers apply over nine pounds per acre[14].

Let's now return to Belle Fourche and revisit John and Mary by taking a look at their dinner menu tonight. Coincidentally, both have a taste for fish and John is planning to thaw some Walleye fillets from an earlier fishing trip and round out his dinner with a mesclun salad and baked potato picked from his own garden. Mary has time to cook tonight too and she picked up some Tilapia, a package of gourmet salad, and potatoes from the local Mega-mart. Both dinners may be delicious yet the impact spheres of just this dinner alone are radically different. John's impact sphere has not grown at all compared to our initial investigation using the MyEnvironment website (Figure 5-1). In contrast Mary's impact sphere (Figure 5-2) is now tremendous in size and includes a great deal of uncertainty relative to food safety.

Is there any doubt that pesticide-free garden produce is truly better for you? Furthermore, is there any question that a

---

[14] China is the 3rd largest importer of foods to the US and provides 70% of our apple juice and nearly 80% of Tilapia consumed in America.

consequence of John and Mary's diverging *personal impact spheres* will be manifested in their long-term health?

So what is a person to do? Certainly not everyone can start fishing, hunting, and gardening, and not everyone has access to a quality farmer's market. Luckily, there are some common sense tips that can help improve food safety in your own home regardless of the food's origin[15].

1. Wash all produce with lots of cold water and scrub as needed.
2. Discard the outer leaves of lettuce, cabbage, and similar vegetables.
3. Since pesticide residues often concentrate in an animal's fat, trim the fat or remove and discard the skin from poultry and fish.

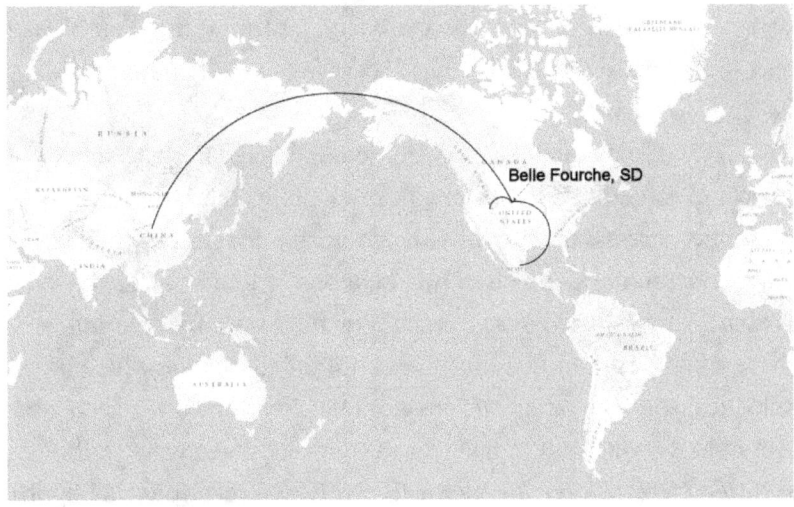

Figure 5- 2 The personal impact sphere of our fictitious character, Mary and her dinner of Tilapia (from China), potatoes (from the US), and salad (from Mexico)

---

[15] Excerpted from the FDA consumer, 1993.

-Introspection-

I was in a cab having one of those interesting conversations with the driver as he shuttled me around Durban, South Africa in 2003. He wanted to talk to me about world peace and having nothing else to do, I engaged with him in a sort of philosophical discussion. His point was well taken; world peace cannot be achieved if each of us does not first seek inner peace.

What does this have to do with food safety and your *personal impact sphere*? Well, actually quite a bit as your *personal impact sphere* includes YOU. What I mean is your lifestyle, personality, and outlook on life can have great consequences on your health as does the food you eat, the water you drink, and the air you breathe. Stress --and how individuals deal with stressful situations-- has been linked to heart disease, asthma, obesity, diabetes, headaches, depression, anxiety, gastrointestinal problems, and according to Dr. Jay Winner[16], perhaps even Alzheimer's disease.

While punctuated or episodic periods of stress have been shown to actually provide some health benefits, chronic or prolonged stress can be deadly. Biologically, humans have been hard-wired to deal with stressful situations or threats through what is commonly referred to as the flight or fight response. During these situations your body receives a jolt of adrenaline which subsides when the threat has passed. In ancient times this response would be very helpful in the event a saber-tooth cat were stalking you (a punctuated event which will end with either you evading the cat until it gives up or... well, you know the gruesome alternative).

---

[16] For more details visit http://www.webmd.com/balance/stress-management/features/10-fixable-stress-related-health-problems or read Dr. Winner's book, *Take the Stress out of Your Life*.

In today's world however the threat or stressor may not subside. Instead, it continues throughout the day for many working in stressful occupations or living in stressful homes. The continued bombardment of your system by adrenaline --resulting in constriction of blood vessels, heightened blood pressure and pulse rates, and redirection of blood circulation away from the digestive system-- is unhealthy and dangerous.

It is interesting that not all individuals respond to a given event in the same way. For some, an event might be perceived as a catastrophe while for others it's simply the way it is and another opportunity to "roll with the punches". There are folks out there who claim to do their best under pressure, but I wonder how long these folks are able to continue "doing their best" when the pressure never ceases.

--

Dogs are pretty much matter-of-fact critters that seem to automatically "roll with the punches". Sure, some exhibit separation anxiety and other idiosyncrasies, but for the most part dogs seem to approach life one moment at a time. Interacting with calm-natured canines can rub off on us as well and research has demonstrated that simply petting a dog lowers one's blood pressure (counteracting the effect of adrenaline) and increases oxytocin production (the hormone oxytocin has the opposite effect of adrenaline and is considered a calming hormone).

Just a few decades ago, no one would have thought something as effortless as petting a dog could have real and quantifiable physical benefits, yet today it is an accepted fact. I suspect there are other benefits dogs provide us that we simply are not yet unaware of.

Chapter 6
-Microwave Mentality-

I consider Gen-X'ers like myself a privileged generation as ours witnessed tremendous fundamental changes in American society. Like most kids from this generation, I grew up in a home with both a mother and father, each of whom maintained traditional roles in the family. My dad brought home the bacon and mom cooked it up, raised us kids, and took care of the entire household.

Growing up in northern Wisconsin, I clearly recall black and white televisions that were built more like a living room cabinet than the entertainment hubs of today. These televisions had a knob prominently located on the front of the box that was used to switch between ABC, CBS, and NBC. That was it --three channels-- and yet everyone seemed to find something worthwhile to watch and even launch arguments over who gets to watch their favorite program next. Television rapidly ensconced itself into American culture and helped accelerate revolutionary changes throughout society. With the invention of "TV dinners" came other changes; the family that once discussed the day's events at the dinner table now became silent observers as they watched newscasters like Walter Cronkite, Eric Sevareid, and David Brinkley deliver the headlines of the day.

And while the Vietnam War raged in Southeast Asia, another war was heating up in the states, the war for civil rights and women's rights[17]. As a result, the face of America's workforce changed, sending rippling aftershocks into the family. Many moms now had a job and a career demanding large portions of their time. With not enough time in the day to prepare the same type of dinner their families had grown accustom to, something had to give. The solution was the mega-mart deli, take-out restaurants, and the microwave oven.

While it may seem innocuous enough, the microwave oven helped cause a radical change in America as it taught us to be impatient and to expect results quickly. I can still remember mail-order catalogs asking their customers to "allow 4-6 weeks for delivery". Today such a lengthy wait would be considered entirely unacceptable. It seems time has been contracted or perhaps it's just that our ability to wait has diminished. Either way, today's American expects --and even demands-- immediate gratification. This demand is catered to and exacerbated by the Internet, social media, and satellite television, while supported by a vast infrastructure of digital high-speed networks and fleets of UPS and FedEx delivery vans.

Admittedly, it is nice to order something from Amazon.com and have it delivered within just a few days. But there are consequences to the *microwave mentality*, namely, a dangerous and growing inability to wait for anything. It has

---

[17] 1963 saw the publication of Betty Friedan's influential book, *The Feminine Mystique* which effectively urged housewives to broaden their role in society.

become far more than simply feeling unhappy when we need to wait. It is a mindset, a paradigm, and even a way of life to assume there should be no waiting. For example, instead of:

✓ Reading a text book and working through scores of exercises to master a topic, today's student expects cliffs notes™, executive summaries, and sound bites, all the while being fast-tracked through their chosen degree program.

✓ Exercising to lose weight and "get into shape", Americans want a pill that will magically dissolve fat and give them six-pack abs.

✓ Focusing all attention on one project, American workers are expected to multitask and complete numerous projects simultaneously[18].

✓ Growing a garden, visiting farmers markets, and selecting a healthy diet, vitamin supplements are increasingly being relied upon. In fact, more than 50% of Americans include vitamin supplements as part of their daily diet, compared to only 40% in 1988.

Are dietary supplements truly good for your health? To comprehensively answer this question would require hundreds of pages of text, tables, and figures, and is beyond the scope of this book. Alternatively, while offering a broad brush overview might require only a sentence or two, it would also fail to provide meaningful information to the reader.

---

[18] As of 2011 the average American's attention span was only five minutes compared to nearly 15 minutes just a decade ago (https://socialtimes.com/tag/attention-span). The consequences of such changes are myriad with some research suggesting creativity is the first of our abilities to suffer from multitasking.

Instead of adopting either of these approaches I have opted to explore just a few of the more popular dietary supplements (Vitamins A, B, C, and D, and Calcium) and provide a summary to better inform the reader and further the discussion of this book[19].

> The second most popular dietary supplement taken in America is the multi-vitamin. Talk about exemplifying the true microwave mentality! While it seems many Americans are concerned about not eating a healthy diet (and that is a good and valid concern), instead of selecting a few key vitamins *they* might be missing out on, they resort to the one-shot wonder pill… the multivitamin.

A Vitamin Summary
-Vitamin A-

Vitamin A is a fat-soluble vitamin found in numerous fruits, vegetables, and dairy products and is most readily available in superfoods like liver, spinach, kale, and carrots. Since it is unlikely that most people will be able to include these superfoods in their diet *every day*, it may be difficult for some to meet the recommended daily allowance (RDA) for vitamin A. Thus, vitamin A supplements *may* be beneficial and according to WebMD, are "likely safe if taken by mouth in amounts less than 10,000 units per day". However, it is important to be aware of the risk of vitamin A overdose --serious liver damage-- and carefully observe the FDA's daily value (DV) benchmark of approximately 5,000 units each day.

-The B Vitamins-

Vitamin B is not just one vitamin but a group of B vitamins better known as thiamine (B1), riboflavin (B2), niacin (B3), pyridoxine (B6), cobalamin (B12), biotin, and folic acid. The

---

[19] The following summaries are provided as a discussion and are not intended to be used as medical advice.

B vitamins can be found in red meat, fish, eggs, and dairy products as well as fortified breakfast cereals. The B vitamins play an important role in the production of red blood cells, proper nervous system function, and even the replication of DNA.

Researching the B vitamins using Internet websites from WebMD and the National Institutes of Health (NIH) suggest the best way to get your daily dose of the B vitamins is through a healthy diet which might begin with a fortified breakfast cereal (25-100% of your B vitamin DV will be met by eating a bowl of cereal, add a cup of milk for an extra 18%) and end with a meal of fish (30-90% DV), beef liver (nearly 1200% DV) or cooked clams (approximately 1400% DV).

-Vitamin C-

Probably the best known vitamin is vitamin C (Ascorbic acid) even though formal scientific research has yet to *prove* any health benefit from taking vitamin C supplements. While it is widely believed that vitamin C supplements increase immunity to the common cold, empirical evidence supporting this is still considered weak[20]. Nonetheless, vitamin C is an important component of healthy living with good sources found in numerous fruits and vegetables, and especially citrus fruits. In fact, it seems pretty easy to develop a diet that will provide all the vitamin C your body needs by including citrus fruits, chili peppers, bell peppers, dark leafy green vegetables (e.g., kale), broccoli, cauliflower, Brussels sprouts, or strawberries. In fact, a serving or two of just one of these foods can easily meet your daily requirement of vitamin C.

---

[20] Just because scientific proof is not available does not mean it is not true. Aerodynamic studies suggest the bumblebee should not be able to fly, yet the fuzzy bee flies very well indeed.

-Calcium-

This mineral plays a key role in bone health and according to WebMD, dietary supplements may be necessary as most US adults do not get enough calcium in their diet. Good sources of dietary calcium include not only dairy products (milk, cheese, and yogurt) but fortified cereals and juices as well. It is interesting that your body needs vitamin D to properly absorb calcium. Furthermore, it is worth knowing that different forms of calcium are used in the manufacture of calcium supplements; calcium carbonate, citrate, gluconate, and lactate. Each of these forms of calcium contains different proportions of what is called elemental calcium (calcium that is available to our bodies). While calcium carbonate (the least expensive form) contains 40% elemental calcium there have been concerns of the carbonate form also containing traces of lead and other heavy metals since the primary source for calcium carbonate is oyster shell (oysters and other shellfish are excellent bio-accumulators of heavy metals and other pollutants)[21].

Calcium citrate is the second most common source used to produce calcium supplements and contains 21% elemental calcium. Calcium citrate is also considered the easiest for the body to absorb. These considerations should be at the forefront when selecting a calcium supplement with particular emphasis placed on the amount of elemental calcium available in each tablet.

-The Sunshine Vitamin-

As already noted, vitamin D plays a crucial and interactive role with calcium in helping to build a healthy skeletal system. Interestingly, nearly 90% of the vitamin D needed by your body is obtained through exposure to the sun. According to WebMD "It's

---

[21] The possibility of contamination should be minimized by the 2007 *Good Manufacturing Practices* document issued by the FDA.

amazing how quickly adequate levels of vitamin D can be restored by sunlight. Just 6 days of casual sunlight exposure without sunscreen can make up for 49 days of no sunlight exposure."

The remaining 10% needed by the body usually comes from eating fatty fish like mackerel and tuna, or fortified dairy products and cereals. In addition, careful use of vitamin D dietary supplements can be used while bearing in mind doses in excess of 4000 IU/day are considered unsafe. Since most vitamin supplements typically contain 400 IU, vitamin D supplements are considered "likely safe when taken in these amounts".

Super food or just a trendy food fad...

Throughout the summary above, did you notice beef liver is cited as a great source of important vitamins (vitamins A, B, D, E, and K) and minerals like iron and copper. It is not just a trendy fad; beef liver is a true super food!

-My Take-

I am a very conservative person who does not gamble on anything. I am also a scientist and through years of training and experience in this field I have become highly skeptical about everything. Have said this, I believe I can take a pragmatic approach to my diet and use of dietary supplements. What follows, is *my* view on vitamin supplements and not a recommendation of what *you* should do as I am not a physician and have no clue about your health condition.

Personally, I take vitamin C supplements daily and have found the Ester-C brand agrees with my digestive system, though I sometimes I have a terrible time swallowing any pill. In this case, I munch down a chewable vitamin C gummy and call it good. I am not convinced taking vitamin C supplements help me avoid the common cold or the flu, but I am also not convinced vitamin C supplements are doing me any harm. For me, the old adage "an ounce of prevention is worth a pound of cure" rings true. The overwhelming majority of my dietary needs are met by a varied diet that usually includes a meat entrée, potatoes or pasta, and a nice salad[22]. My approach is certainly not for everyone but it seems to work for me.

--

The *microwave mentality* does not only apply to our *personal* impatience, demand for immediate gratification, and bad dietary habits, it has become so prolific and so ubiquitous that it is part of American government, business, and industry. Our microwave mentality is the reason we have a thriving fast food market, oodles of plastic products, packaging, and "dinner ware", and is a driving force behind a serious global issue; food security.

I attended a conference just a few years back where one of the speakers listed what he considered the many advances of the multinational chemical and agricultural biotechnology company that he worked for (we will call it CABCO). One of these was CABCO's success with genetically modified organisms (GMO) and the speaker proudly proclaimed that CABCO has saved the world!

Let's back this train up a bit and make it clear that GMO products have not saved the world and likely will never save the world. On the contrary, mounting evidence shows consuming GMO-based foods (corn, soybeans, and canola being prime examples) can results in irreparable organ damage, immune system disorders, and infertility[23]. Ironically, the promise of GMO

---

[22] For a more detailed discussion I suggest reading *The End of Illness* by David B. Agus and *In Defense of Food* by Michael Pollan.

[23] See the 2009 report from the American Academy of Environmental Medicine at http://www.aaemonline.org/gmopressrelease.html

products to increase yields while decreasing the use of pesticides simply has not happened. What has happened instead is GMO crop yields have been no better than yields from traditional varieties, as GMO crop yields have not only been erratic but frequently exhibit increased water demands as well.

More critically, over the same time period (1994-2010) that saw an increased use of GMO corn and soybean varieties by US farmers also saw a concomitant increase in applied herbicide volume across the nation. Indeed the USDA reports a 30% increase in herbicide application on corn and soybean crops while approximately 70-90% of the corn and soybeans crops are GMO products. Proponents of GMO have argued the increase in pesticide use is due to farmers who use non-GMO varieties while others point to the rapid evolution of super pests that all producers are now contending with.

The bigger issue surrounding GMO's has nothing to do with crop yields or herbicide application but global food security (the assurance of the availability of food in the future). Corn is arguably the most important crop in the entire world and for this reason will be the focus of this section of the book.

Corn has been given the scientific species name *Zea mays*. There are nine subspecies of *Zea mays* including popcorn, flour corn, dent corn (field corn), and sweet corn. There are approximately 120 cultivated varieties (cultivars) of sweet corn and over 70 cultivars of field corn currently available to the US farm market alone. The number of corn cultivars worldwide is tremendous.

What this means is *Zea mays* is a genetically diverse species and even though many of its cultivars are hybrids, the biodiversity, or rather the genetic variability within this plant is rich[24]. While most GMO corn is the field corn type, not all field corn cultivars are a GMO. Furthermore, it is important to appreciate the fact there is more genetic variability within non-GMO *Zea mays* than there is within GMO-based *Zea mays*. While genetic variability is important for a number of reasons, it is specifically applicable here because high genetic variability helps ensure the survival of a species following an epidemic or plague.

To put this into context, the Black Death (caused by a variant of the *Yersinia pestis* bacterium) killed nearly 30% of the world's population and approximately 60% of the population of Europe over a period of just four years. But not everyone in Europe died even if they lived in the same village as others who become infected with the plague. The reason for this apparent oddity has been speculated about for some time, with some hypothesizing that survivors had somehow been immune to the Black Death. The source of their immunity was simply their unique genetic makeup and nothing more. Recent empirical support for this notion was published in the Proceedings of the National Academy of Sciences of the United States of America (2014) describing the immune systems of two genetically distinct populations in Europe[25]. The take-home message here is this: high genetic variability is critical to the long term survival of a species.

A conspicuous problem for corn growers is the fact corn is a wind pollinated crop. If one farmer chooses to grow a GMO corn cultivar while his neighbor grows a non-GMO cultivar, it is not only possible but highly likely the two will cross-pollinate. This is

---

[24] Visit the Maize Genetics and Genomics Database at http://1289www.maizegdb.org/ to see just how diverse this plant really is.

[25] For more details read *Convergent evolution in European and Rroma populations reveals pressure exerted by plague on Toll-like receptors*, Hafid Laayouni, et al., PNAS, DOI: 10.1073/pnas.1317723111

known as pollen drift and is especially concerning for seed corn growers as their crop will be contaminated by the GMO crop. In theory, we will see fewer and fewer pure non-GMO cultivars of corn in the world and as a result, a reduction in genetic variability.

Returning to the topic of global food security, just imagine the consequences of a pest (insect, bacteria, virus, or super pest) that learns how to (i.e., evolves to) exploit a vulnerability in the corn's new, *simplified* genetic makeup. While this would <u>not</u> spell the end of the world as we know it --thanks to places like Norway's Svalbard Global Seed Vault-- it could produce a global corn-famine that would lead to countless deaths (especially in developing countries that rely far more on corn as a primary food source) and significant economic losses.

-*Connecting Threads*-

Since the overwhelming majority of GMO corn cultivars are a type of field corn, do we really have anything to worry about relative to our own diet? Initially this question seems to take the wind out of our sails until we better understand that field corn <u>is</u> a common component of our diet.

Most field corn is used for animal feed and increasingly, bio-fuel production, and is not a directly considered part of the American diet. When used as an animal feed, it is important that we understand farmers, ranchers, and feedlot operators have numerous regulations that govern the proper care of livestock (it used to be called animal husbandry) and ultimately, the people who will purchase and consume the meat produced by these animals.

> Beef does not need to be *finished* using field corn or any grain at all for that matter. If you are like me you may find grass-fed beef a healthier and yet equally delicious alternative. What's more, grass-fed beef is rich in Omega-3 fatty acids.

In this case, we are not consuming field corn directly but instead consume meat that is produced (or more correctly, *finished*) using field corn.

Secondly, GMO corn is used to produce high fructose corn syrup (HFCS) which is consumed in huge quantities all across this nation (about 64 pounds of pure HFCS per person each year). The concerns about HFCS are myriad and likely do not require any further elaboration other than to say we would be healthier as a nation by reducing our total sugar consumption and especially simple sugars obtained from HFCS.

Third, field corn --recall that 70-90% of field corn grown in the US is GMO-based-- is used to produce breakfast cereal. While the benefits of fortified breakfast cereals (described earlier) are clear, it is nearly certain that all breakfast cereal containing corn uses GMO corn <u>unless</u> the product is labelled "USDA certified organic" or "non-GMO".

Lastly, consider the consumer pyramid (Figure 6-1) shown below. Notice the highest quality corn products are designated for human consumption (tier one). Foods of somewhat lower quality or grading are considered suitable for animal feed (tier two) while the lowest quality corn products are fed to animals "not intended for human consumption", in other words, our dogs[26].

This brings us nearly full circle and begs us to recall the rising rates of cancer and other disorders being observed today in our dogs (see chapter one).

Who is to blame for these problems? Is it the US government, global capitalism, or the agriculture industry? You may be shocked to learn the answer is none of the above. In fact you do not need to look any further than your own chair because

---

[26] This is yet another good reason to use entirely grain-free dog food.

what got us into all these troubles is our own expediency, our *microwave mentality*. It is the same demand for immediate "everything" that has resulted in a proliferation of plastics and chemicals promising to make life easier and give us "something" for nothing; growing crops without weeding, getting thin without exercising, and becoming rich without working.

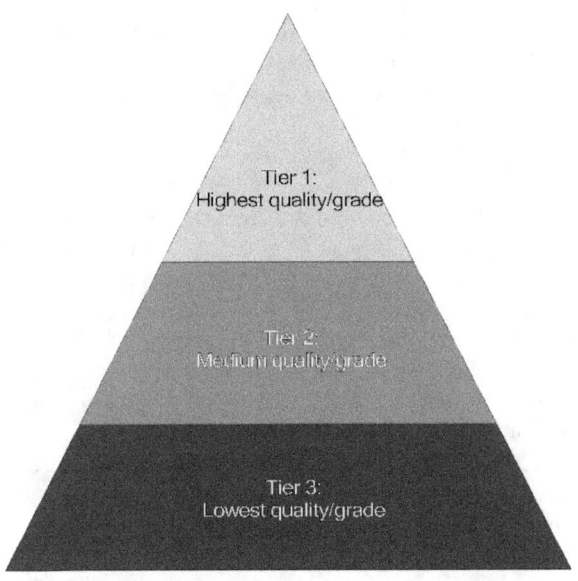

Figure 6- 1 The consumer pyramid provides a generalized overview of how food is graded and consumed in America

Faith in a Seed...

In 1996 the final essays of Henry David Thoreau were published in an anthology titled *Faith in a Seed*. The title of this delightful book provides plenty to contemplate, especially as it relates to global food security.

While we may revel in our technological advances, the fact remains today, just as much as it ever has, that agriculture is the keystone or foundation of human civilization. Anthropologists tell us by 7000 BC (during the Neolithic revolution), man possessed the skills necessary to alter his nomadic, hunter/gatherer lifestyle and settle down into what would become villages and towns of sometimes 1000 or more inhabitants. Without even the most rudimentary knowledge of agronomy, human civilization could not have evolved beyond the hunter/gatherer. One may argue it was the cultivation of crops that allowed for the survival of cities and ultimately the vast divisions of labor we see today.

Farming has always been a difficult yet rewarding life, but the romanticized notions of today's farmer may be more fiction than fact. Indeed, the great majority of America's farmland is managed under what is known as *industrial agriculture*. This chemically-intensive and petroleum-dependent form of food production arose following World War II. Today, industrial agriculture is under scrutiny and increasingly viewed as an unsustainable form of food production because of problems associated with[1]:

- Increasing pesticide use
- The use of antibiotics in feed lots
- The use of rendered meats as cattle feed

My grandfather was a dairy farmer and his favorite animal on the planet was the cow. He was heartbroken when his barn burned following a lightning strike and much of his herd perished. His sorrow was a sincere loss for these wonderful animals. If my grandfather were alive today I wonder what he would think about *farming* today.

1- For a more detailed discussion, visit the Union of Concerned Scientists website at http://www.ucsusa.org/food_and_agriculture/our-failing-food-system/industrial-agriculture/

Chapter 7
-Point-

Legends abound explaining how dogs came to be man's best friend. In nearly every story, the <u>first</u> dog (proto-dog) befriends someone in need, helps them, and then promises to remain loyal forever. Each of these stories suggests dogs chose to be with us and stay with us. Interestingly, recent studies generally support these legends and suggest the earliest dogs may truly have chosen to live with people[27].

Today, dogs can be found in nearly 50% of American households and for an overwhelming majority of those Americans, the dog is a member of the family. He takes part in family vacations, portraits, and frequently finds something beneath the Christmas tree just for him.

Because of their close kinship with us, dogs are <u>inadvertently exposed to the same</u> environment we face each day:

---

[27] Read *Dogs: A Startling New Understanding of Canine Origin, Behavior & Evolution* by Raymond and Lorna Coppinger (2001)

air pollution, water contamination, and unhealthy diets. In essence, dogs live within the same *impact sphere* we have created for ourselves (see chapter five). As a result, we are observing numerous health parallels between humans and dogs (see chapters one and two).

Cancer is the second leading cause of death in the US, accounting for just over 574,000 deaths in 2010 or approximately 23% of all deaths. These figures describe human mortality and are strikingly similar to canine cancer deaths which account for 25% of deaths according to Morris Animal foundation estimates.

While genetics play a role in an individual's cancer susceptibility, the environment or rather your *personal impact sphere* likely contributes far more significantly. According to the American Cancer Society, numerous carcinogens are regularly found in the average US household including radon and radio frequency radiation (cellular phones and smart meters installed to measure your household's use of natural gas, electricity, and water[28]) . While the jury may still be out concerning other *possible* carcinogens like recombinant bovine growth hormone (rBGH[29]), aspartame (an artificial sweetener better known as NutraSweet® and Equal®), xenoestrogens (see chapter two), and GMO-based corn products, a rational approach for the American consumer is to eliminate these products from our shopping lists until conclusive proof is in hand clearly demonstrating their safety. I am sure you will agree the alternative (i.e., continue using these products until they have been banned) is just too risky.

---

[28] See the World Health Organization's International Agency for Research on Cancer (IARC) for a more detailed discussion.

[29] rBGH is administered to dairy cows to increase milk production. There is a long-standing concern that residues of this hormone, which may be found in milk and other dairy products, could be unhealthy for humans to consume.

The list of carcinogens grows even larger when we leave our homes and explore workplace carcinogens. It's here that many Americans are exposed to a host of carcinogenic chemicals like acrylamide (used in a wide variety of industries ranging from paper and pulp manufacture, to food processing, plastics, and even textile production), benzene (exposure is very common at any gasoline-related industry), perfluorooctanic acid (PFOA; used to produce Teflon®), and formaldehyde (widely used in the building materials industry).

Whether you work in one of the industries mentioned above or not, there is little escape from environmental carcinogens today. Just breathing carries certain cancer risks especially if the air contains gasoline or diesel exhaust fumes[30].

--

Heart disease is the leading cause of death in the US and diabetes comes in at number seven. Together, these conditions account for 27% of all deaths and share an interesting connection; both are related to obesity and being overweight. This is a significant connection considering nearly 70% of Americans are considered overweight or obese[31]. What is even more interesting is this number has been increasing over the past few decades, even though this same time period might be considered the "healthy diet enlightenment" era.

According to a recent survey, dogs are following a similar trend as more than half our dogs are considered overweight. The culprit for both man and his best friends is an unhealthy lifestyle; we simply eat too much and exercise too little.

---

[30] Visit the American Cancer Society's website at
http://www.cancer.org/cancer/cancercauses/othercarcinogens/pollution/index

[31] Source: Centers for Disease Control and Prevention (CDC),
http://www.cdc.gov/nchs/fastats/overwt.htm

According to the USDA the total calories consumed by each American has increased nearly 25% since 1970. A more telling characterization of our eating habits goes beyond the amount of food on each plate[32] and instead describes the types of foods we are consuming. Indeed, the same USDA report shows dairy product consumption has declined steadily since 1950 while the use of additional fats and oils (principally salad and cooking oils) has increased nearly 70%. What's more, consumption of sweeteners has increased 40% even with a *reduction* in cane and beet sugar usage that is more than made up for by an astonishing 800% increase in the consumption of corn sweeteners such as high-fructose corn syrup (HFCS).

The solution certainly seems simple; eat less (and eat better, more healthy foods) and exercise more to better balance caloric intake with output. In reality however, it's not that simple and here's why. According to the US Bureau of Labor Statistics (BLS), there are nearly three Americans working in white collar jobs for every one working in a blue collar job. That means 75% of America's workforce is getting very little physical exercise while at their workplace. Compare that to a century ago, when pre-industrial agriculture farming constituted 1/3rd of the entire US labor force[33].

Office jobs are not trivial by any means and frequently place tremendous stress burdens on the worker. What's more, many of today's office workers inadvertently (and perhaps unwillingly) take their stress burden home, resulting in long-term

---

[32] For a fascinating perspective on diet, read David Ludwig and Mark Friedman's Journal of the American Medical Association (JAMA) paper *Increasing Adiposity: Consequence or Cause of Overeating?*

[33] This was the pre-industrialized era of agriculture when the average farm size was only 138 acres.

elevation of cortisol levels (adrenaline) which can lead to any number of health problems such as high blood pressure, heart attack, and stroke (see chapter 5 for an additional discussion).

It's curious to wonder how accurate the estimate of calories burned actually is. I say this, because the brain is an extremely energy consumptive organ --using 20-30% of total calories burned each day-- with recent research suggesting more challenging mental tasks burn even more calories just as does increased physical exertion. An even more interesting fact is that the brain really is a *sugar junkie* and while not entirely conclusive, studies from around the world are indicating that eating sugar-rich foods may actually improve performance on more mentally challenging tasks. Perhaps then, the imbalance between caloric intake and output is not as great as previously thought. Furthermore, our nation's increase in sugar consumption may be explained, at least in part, by a parallel change in America's workforce and a craving for sugar-rich, brain-candy foods to better fuel our minds. However, even if our brains are calling for us to devour sugar-rich foods, the source of those sugars (GMO-based HFCS) is likely doing us more harm than good.

An undeniable fact remains; our bodies require <u>physical</u> exercise to remain healthy. It's not simply burning calories that's important, but the physical activity that exercises your heart and muscles while building a strong body and burning some calories along the way.

Getting good exercise may be more easily said that done however as many American's are finding it increasingly difficult to locate safe and accessible outlets for exercise. An interesting hypothesis has appeared relatively recently suggesting obesity and being overweight is far more complicated than the simplistic solution "eat less, exercise more" suggests. Indeed, a more holistic perspective of the problem includes examining the neighborhood and community in which we live. Like the EPA's MyEnvironment, this approach explores the availability of the ordinary exercise outlets many of us take for granted. Things like sidewalks, parks, green space, hiking and walking trails, as well as access to fresh food grocers, farmer's markets, and medical care. The term used to describe these features is the "built environment" and the term encapsulates not only the presence of features but safe accessibility as well as connectivity[34]. Research indicates having a park within a kilometer (0.6 miles) of your home increases the likelihood of getting adequate exercise by nearly 20%. Taking this a step further, these findings also suggest the likelihood a person will walk out their door and follow a sidewalk to a park or walking trail to get some exercise is much better than if the only way to get to a park is by driving or walking along the curb of a street. If this scenario is compounded further still by a fear for one's safety, the likelihood of that person getting exercise diminishes even more.

Another legitimate consideration influencing a person's health potential is their economic status. We have probably all heard the somewhat cynical statement that only the wealthy can afford to be healthy, but there is certainly some truth to this. It is expensive to belong to a fitness club, buy a home in "better neighborhoods" (which have improved access to walking trails, city parks, etc.), and visit a doctor for regular wellness exams. Beyond these fairly obvious economic divergences there are also more subtle disparities; for example let's consider a scenario where a well-intentioned lower or middle-class parent wants to provide a healthy breakfast for their family. While shopping up and down the

[34] Wildlife biologists have considered habitat connectivity for decades to better understand and manage populations of threatened and endangered species. The impact of habitat fragmentation is well recognized as is the importance of migration or movement corridors connecting two otherwise fragmented habitat areas.

breakfast cereals aisle, this parent will be bombarded by Madison Avenue marketing and a nearly overwhelming selection of products. But this parent is resolute and having done some homework has decided to check into fortified, organic, non-GMO cereals. This greatly reduces the playing field to only a handful of selections each costing around $0.44 per ounce. Glancing to the left or right of these options, this parent compares the good-for-you cereal with similar non-organic options which ring up at $0.09 per ounce. Noticing the long list of groceries still on the list, which box of cereal do you really think will end up in the shopping cart? Moreover, which one would you choose or even more to the point, which one do you already choose?

This scenario is not unusual and certainly not limited to the breakfast cereal aisle. In fact, I personally have not made it a point to purchase only organic cereals. This does not mean all other options are necessarily bad, as we *can* eat healthy even without seeing a certified organic label. In breakfast cereals, I personally avoid any of those containing corn because without the certified organic seal, I will surely be consuming a GMO product. But GMO has not infiltrated the wheat, barley, and oat markets yet (primarily because the genome of these plants has not yet been successfully mapped or in the case for wheat, the GM products have not yet been approved by the FDA) and so an appealing, fortified breakfast cereal made from one of these grains is often my first choice. Next, I look at the ingredients and while it is nearly impossible to entirely omit sweeteners from cereals (we are told many would be unpalatable otherwise), we can still select cereals with minimal additional sweeteners that use cane sugar instead of HFCS. This approach, I have found, can be agreeable for both your body and your bank account.

--

Earlier in this chapter you may recall the statistic that nearly 70% of Americans are considered overweight or obese. While a similar trend is seen in America's dog community, it is not a perfect parallel and justifiably, one might ask "why aren't 70% of our dogs overweight just like us?" First, understand the parallel that does exist is actually pretty substantial even if it does not represent a perfect relationship. Second, I believe there are several good reasons why a greater proportion of people are overweight relative to the proportion of overweight dogs.

- ✓ Dog food does not contain HFCS.
- ✓ Dog food does not contain sugar.
- ✓ While there are numerous similarities between a dog's diet and ours, dogs are far more carnivorous and enjoy a diet lower in carbohydrates than we do (I am certainly not suggesting we need to invent a new *canine diet fad* as humans have their own unique digestive system and dietary needs).
- ✓ Dogs do very well with a diet containing as much as 30% fat. Hence the increased use of fats in our diets (and the table scraps shared with our dogs) may actually be healthy for dogs but not for us.
- ✓ By their nature, most dogs like to run and actually enjoy exercise.
- ✓ It is far easier to put your dog on a diet than to put yourself on a diet (most dogs have not figured out how to open refrigerators and help themselves to a midnight snack).
- ✓ Dogs do not live as long as us and simply do not have as much time to become obese.

To some readers, the outlook may appear gloomy. Yet there is plenty each of us can do that will truly make a difference not only in our own individual lives but collectively, for the lives of all Americans.

You have almost certainly heard the slogan "reduce, reuse, recycle". These three simple words --and their underlying actions-- raised awareness and galvanized the nation to help develop a very successful waste reduction program. A solution to the overall health problems we are facing in America is actually very similar and needs to begin at the grassroots level: the individual. Here are some recommendations.

✓ Grow your own organic vegetable and fruit garden.
✓ Enroll in Bountiful Baskets[35] (or similar food co-op) to obtain seasonally fresh fruits and vegetables with an organically grown option.
✓ Visit local Farmer's Markets to purchase produce you may not be able to grow successfully in your home garden.
✓ Use your consumer buying power at the grocery store to purchase healthy foods. Remember, the Mega-marts are selling to you and you have every right to spend your hard earned money on what you want to buy. Believe it or not, the Mega-marts *will* notice a change in consumer spending habits and in turn alter their buying practices to better cater to the shopper and get you to spend more of your money at their store.
✓ Whenever possible buy organic, certified non-GMO produce, wild- caught fish, grass-fed beef, and free-range poultry.
✓ Get some physical exercise every day.

---

[35] The importance of seeking seasonally fresh produce should not be overlooked and this is the success behind the food co-ops. Visit http://www.bountifulbaskets.org/ to sign up.

✓ Get a dog. In the book *The End of Illness*, Dr. David B. Agus suggests getting a dog to help improve your health. The connections are fascinating as research has demonstrated that simply petting a dog can reduce stress and lower blood pressure. Another wonderful thing your dog will do for you is get you into a regular routine that includes exercise (i.e., walking the dog).

Chapter 8
-Counter Point-

On September 27th, 1962, Rachel Carson's *Silent Spring* was published. The now classic text scrutinized the negative effects humans have on their world, highlighting in particular the impact pesticides have on the environment. The book's sole focus was not DDT (dichlorodiphenyltrichloroethane) however, but the impact of pesticides in general. As a result of Carson's book --along with studies dating back to the 1940's-- DDT was banned in the US in 1972.

Even before the publication of *Silent Spring* there had been considerable debate about the environment and to what extent our actions impact the world around us. Surely, no sensible person today would argue we do not have the *capacity* to pollute our planet. However, in light of current laws regulating the use of chemicals and industrial emissions, a myriad of monitoring programs, as well as the complexities of truly comprehending our ecosystem, it is often unclear precisely how (and sometimes if) we are affecting our world.

Every issue seems to have two highly polarized perspectives along with others whose viewpoint lies along a continuum somewhere between the poles. For many, DDT is without question a terrible chemical. Others however, are quick to point out that banning DDT caused millions of human deaths in developing countries where DDT had been used to control mosquitos and the malaria-causing *Plasmodium* parasite they carried. I am not arguing either viewpoint is perfectly correct but simply pointing out that very few global or even national issues are ever clear cut and without legitimate debate.

The issues described in *Silent Spring* seem almost simplistic in contrast to those being faced today. It is not only pesticides but all manner of pollutants that are contaminating our environment and our bodies. It's the chemical industry, plastics, hormone-mimicking substances, and genetically modified organisms (the list goes on) which were developed to improve our lives but may be inadvertently destroying us. There is still no smoking gun that has been found but instead an extremely complex web of interactions that very much includes us, the decisions we make, and our consumer demands and expectations.

I believe the problem has become so complex that even our most brilliant scientists and our most powerful supercomputers will be unable to comprehend it or analyze it, and as a result, we may have little hope of arriving at a solution. Yet there are many who will argue there is no problem at all, but instead only a fictional dilemma created by environmentalists.

The basis for the latter viewpoint is not without merit as the expert opinion of physicians and scientists is not unanimous on any of the issues raised in this book. To further add confusion there is even disagreement between government agencies and the documents they publish (e.g., vitamin recommendations made by the USDA and FDA do not always agree) just as there is also disagreement between government agencies and industry regarding the safety of various chemicals as well as the effect of certain manufacturing processes.

I have been very careful to use what I consider authoritative sources throughout this book. Even so, the best facts and figures I have been able to provide were usually approximations as the single *correct* answer was simply not available. But exact answers are frequently unavailable because:

- ✓ **Reality**. It truly is difficult to get exact counts or measurement of certain events or observations (for example, the exact total acreage sown as GMO-corn (if you think about it, it's actually quite difficult to measure the area of any real property hence the ubiquitous use of "more or less" (MOL) by the real estate industry)).
- ✓ **Shelter**. In a nation of litigation, it is considered far safer to report approximations, as there is plenty of *wiggle-room* built into an estimate.
- ✓ **Statistics**. Many of the figures we read today were not derived from counts or direct measurements but through statistical analysis of sample data. These figures are then extrapolated (or interpolated) using various measures of central tendency to produce an estimate that is intended to be descriptive of a larger population within a given confidence interval.
- ✓ **Bias**. It is in the interest of certain parties not to disclose specific data since doing so might incriminate themselves or sever an important relationship.

In the end, we do not need exact figures anyway. Instead, what is really important is recognizing the forest and not just counting trees. Put another way, a critical part of this book is seeing the big picture and the over-arching truths suggested by the estimates and approximations.

It has become brutally apparent to me we are not living in Pollyanna-Ville or the Garden of Eden. Instead, our environment -- however broadly you wish to define it-- has become a dangerous place to live, especially for those with allergies, sensitivities (or hyper-sensitivity) to specific substances, or a genetic predisposition for a health condition or disease.

While very real, this danger is subtle, pervasive, and complex. Due to its complex nature, eliminating the danger will be extremely difficult and probably costly. I am convinced this danger stems from our microwave mentality and we ourselves are much to blame for creating this monster. It's the artificial, chemical concoctions we eat and drink every day. It's the preservatives that help foods last longer and the additives that make foods sweeter, all for a nation where plastics have nearly eliminated wood, steel, glass, and tin, to be competitive in a world marketplace where the winner gets… what?

The solution is not another government program or additional laws and regulations. Instead the solution will need to be a holistic one where each and every one of us takes personal responsibility for our own health and well-being and that of our children. It will require an eyes wide open awareness of our environment beginning with an assessment of your *personal impact sphere*. Following the assessment you will almost surely realize the need to change your lifestyle as knowledge alone will be of no benefit without action. For each individual, this will be the most difficult part of "living healthy" because it will mean more work (physical exercise and rejection of the microwave mentality) and more of your discretionary income spent on healthy food options. These individual difficulties will be the primary reason why the declining health trend we see across this nation today will not only continue but almost certainly grow.

Our destiny does not need to be so gloomy however. If each of us takes responsibility for our own health and acts upon that knowledge by leveraging our consumer spending power, real changes will result. Shop smart, eat healthy, and exercise your body. This is not rocket science, but actually common sense principles that have been stifled though decades of choosing the fast and easy path. Decades of core changes that created a society with a microwave mentality. The solution will not be instant but it needs to begin somewhere, with someone, today.

Changing our spending habits will not be the sole solution to all our problems but it most certainly is part of the solution. Given the breadth and magnitude of problems we are facing today, similar core value changes[36] will need to be made by industry and our government as well. The likelihood of these changes being realized may seem minuscule until you recall the collective power of one. Here are some examples of how the collective power of one can really make a difference.

Table 8- 1 Examples of how you can apply your power of one

One hour spent reading and researching each week
One letter sent to your elected officials
One letter sent to a company you have decided to no longer patronize
One letter sent to a company whose ecologically conscious practices has earned your business
One vote on Election Day
One dollar spent on a healthy choice

---

[36] These core value changes include putting people above profit and embracing the system of governance envisioned by America's founding fathers; one that is truly of the people, by the people, and for the people.

Chapter 9
-Conclusions -

They say dogs were sent to earth to teach us something. If you do not believe this --and if you have had a dog-- then think back to a day before you got your dog. Think back and try to recall your life's values and goals at that time in your past. Now, fast forward and recall to mind the values and goals you hold important today. If you are being honest with yourself I doubt you will find your values and goals have remained the same. Instead, like many other things, your current values and goals have changed. You have matured perhaps or re-evaluated what's important to you. Why? Well, many things can change us (arguably, every life experience changes us and helps to form and re-form our personal paradigm) and sharing our lives with a dog is part of life's journey. Sometimes a dog's impact on our lives will be subtle and nearly transparent. Other times, a dog's effect will be truly profound. Don't you think your dog changed your life for the better?

The first dog you read about in this book was our first Great Pyrenees, Romy. Romy's love and gentle-nature truly provided me with a glimpse into the meaning of life. Like a body that is nourished by food and water, the soul is nourished by love. Not just receiving love but giving love too. Hence, I have come to understand that a soul can grow strong and vigorous or it can wither. Through Romy's life with us I think I have a better idea of what it's going to take to reach heaven's pearly gates and it has nothing to do with a career, money, or any other measure of status commonly accepted in American society today.

Julie helped us better understand dogs as she showed us how they are similar to us and how they are different from us. Because she has a somewhat dominant personality, living with Julie required us to improve our communication with dogs, assert our role as "alpha", and practice being a "benevolent dictator". Julie is still with us today and enjoys being a true member of our family.

Like our very own child, we knew Simon pretty much from conception and even have ultrasound photos of this wonderful dog. Simon taught us how to find joy in everything. Shortly after he passed away a close friend of ours expressed condolences and (knowing of his seizures) told us how truly sorry she was hearing about the problems we experienced with Simon. I took absolutely no offense to such heart-felt and sincere condolences but her words made me think. Simon died at the age of 4 ½ and if I count up all the bad days he had (the days he had seizures) then 99% of his life were days filled with happiness and joy (how many of us can claim such an average). I count only those days when he had seizures as his bad days (or painful, unhappy days) and if you do not agree with my calculation, then it is clear, you never met Simon. He found joy in greeting us each morning, eating his meals, taking walks, visiting neighbors, visiting livestock, visiting school children (Simon was a reading "therapy" dog for local elementary schools), taking trips, and stealing biscuits. In fact, I can honestly say I cannot recall a time when he actually got into trouble. He was easy to train and eager to make us all happy.

He <u>did</u> make us happy and it seemed no one could resist smiling and falling in love with Simon. Simon was an individual with a serious and significant health condition, one that ultimately cost him his life far earlier than should have been. Yet, he lived his life in utter happiness and joy, truly enjoying each and every moment he spent here on earth.

Surely some will say that I am being overly-anthropomorphic and that Simon's *apparent* happiness is entirely attributable to a dog's lack of self-awareness (he simply did not know he was sick). Real "dog people" know this is not true however. Dogs are not the dumb beasts many would like us to think they are. Dogs are family, and like all families we are bound to be together again in heaven[37].

Not everyone has a Romy, Julie, or Simon but has had similar experiences with other wonderful dogs. While our dogs may help each of us learn specific life lessons, I believe there is also a collective and broader message to be heard. If we simply step back and observe what is going on around us, the ultimate message we need to understand is a warning that something is wrong with our environment, something that is very complex and very complicated. Put another way, how can one rationalize that everything is okay. How can one imagine there is no truth behind the trends and correlations described in this book and other books like this one?

---

[37] I encourage you to read Friar Jack Wintz's book, *I will see you in Heaven.*

Through the short lives our dogs spend so closely with us they may be revealing the effect of environmental dangers in a way that becomes easier for us to understand. I write this because sometimes we fail to see --and comprehend what we are seeing-- if we are too close to the problem. However, when we step back, many problems come clearly into focus. In this way, the slight separation between people and dogs may be just enough to allow us to focus and recognize a broad, environmental problem. The separation I am referring to is first the obvious separation between man and dog (as distinct species), as well as the fact a dog's life differs from ours and its lifespan is shorter than ours. As a result of the latter separation, many of us witness *firsthand* the problems with cancer, pollutants, and an unhealthy environment and hopefully begin making the connection between the health of our dogs and our own health. It was Julius Caesar who said "Experience is the teacher of all things" and unfortunately this remains true even where tragedy, sadness, and suffering are the lessons to be learned.

--

In chapter one, I admonished you, the reader, to be far more critical of the truisms so readily broadcast across the Internet, television, and media outlets today. Through the balance of this book, I attempted to share reliable data, information --and sometimes my personal perspectives-- concerning environmental health issues and the subsequent or potential consequences an unhealthy environment might have on both us and our dogs. I do not claim to have provided a comprehensive treatment on each topic and indeed, that was never the intent of this book. Instead, in just 70 terse pages, I feel I have provided a wealth of information and references to stimulate your thinking and aid you in *your* future research. What is perhaps most important though, is that somehow, you are better for having read this book. Live well!

Index

References

Throughout this book I have provided context specific references as footnotes to aid the reader and provide you an opportunity to learn more about a given topic or issue. Even though all resources are important, not all were footnoted. To further aid the reader an on-line reference resource is provided that includes numerous URL's links, documents, and reports. The reader is encouraged to visit http://bit.ly/CanaryThatBarked to use these resources.

www.ingramcontent.com/pod-product-compliance
Lightning Source LLC
Chambersburg PA
CBHW060338290526
45793CB00003B/662